Standard Christmas Program Book

compiled by

Pat Fittro

**STANDARD
PUBLISHING**
Cincinnati, Ohio

Permission is granted to reproduce this material for ministry purposes only—not for resale.

The Standard Publishing Company, Cincinnati, Ohio
A division of Standex International Corporation
© 1998 by The Standard Publishing Company

ISBN 0-7847-0815-0

Contents

Easy

Welcome

Iris Gray Dowling

We welcome you to our church
   today,
We have a song to sing and a
   piece to say;
You can sit quietly in your pews,
We'll tell you the Christmas news.

My Christmas Wish

Margaret Primrose

I wish you happiness,
   Joy and love,
For these are the gifts
   God sends from above.

Merry Christmas!

All Creation Tells

Kimberly Seevers

Let every star shine so bright
   When Christmas comes.
Let every nation be at peace
   When Christmas comes.
Let every family sing joyfully
   When Christmas comes.
Let every heart desire to worship
   When Christmas comes.

Joyful

Dolores Steger

Joyful as the angels,
The shepherds, wise men, too,
May you be this Christmas.
That's my wish for you.

Our Hope

Iris Gray Dowling

For those who feel no joy
There's hope in what I say;
"Jesus Christ has come to earth,
What a happy Christmas Day!"

Twinkle

Dolores Steger

Twinkle, twinkle Christmas star,
Shine for children near and far,
Spread your light upon the earth,
For all to know of Jesus' birth.

A Wonderful Story

Margaret Primrose

Angels sang about Jesus
   While shepherds saw His glory.
Wise men followed a star.
   What a wonderful story!

Praise Him Always

Kimberly Seevers

"Praise Him!" said the angels.
"Praise Him!" said the kings.
"Praise Him!" shouted the
  shepherds
Down on bended knees.

God Sent His Son

Iris Gray Dowling

God sent His Son to Bethlehem,
Filled with everlasting love.
So people's hearts would turn to
  Him,
This Savior who came from
Heaven above.

What Angels Said

Cora M. Owen

Angels said He'd come to earth,
With a lowly humble birth.
Angels said His name would be,
Jesus, Who would die for me.

Listen to the Carolers

Iris Gray Dowling

I heard the carolers once again,
Singing joyous Christmas songs.
I listened to their words—
I know that Jesus came to right
  sin's wrongs.

Give a Cheer

Dolores Steger

Bells and carols now I hear
And know that Christmas time is
  near.
It's Jesus' birthday; give a cheer.
I wish that it would last all year.

Thanks to Baby Jesus

Margaret Primrose

Our thanks to baby Jesus
Never needs to end
Because He is also God
And wants to be our friend.

Finding the King

Margaret Primrose

Shine and shimmer, big bright star
Leading wise men from afar,
May we also find the King.
May we, too, our offering bring.

A Story to Remember

Margaret Primrose

Long, long ago and far, far away
Christ came to earth that first
  Christmas Day,
And each year we hear the story
  retold
For it's wonderfully true, and it
  never grows old.

Celebrate

Iris Gray Dowling

I want to hear the choirs sing
  Their merry songs on Christmas
  Day;
I want to hear the hand bells ring
  To celebrate Jesus' birthday.

God's Gift to Us All

Iris Gray Dowling

Listen while I read God's holy
  Word,
  And tell of the gift God sent to
  us all—
Jesus was born as a babe in
  Bethlehem,
  Not in a fancy church, but a
  cattle stall.
(Read Luke 2:7.)

He Is With Us

Kimberly Seevers

There is wonder in this season
As families join in peace
Remembering the birth of the
Mighty king of kings.
There is comfort in our hearts
Songs of joy everlasting
As the Father's plan unfolds and
Immanuel is with us.

We Love You, Jesus

Margaret Primrose

Sleep, baby Jesus.
  Rest in the hay.
You came to show us
  God's holy way.

Often I wonder
  How it can be
He has such love
  For children like me.

Wake, baby Jesus,
  Open Your eyes.
Smile at Your mother
  And the blue skies.

God in His heavens
  Sent us His Son.
We love You, Jesus.
  You are that One.

*(May be sung to the tune of
"Rockaby, Baby.")*

6

Medium

Message of the Bells

Cora M. Owen

The bells give forth a lovely
    sound,
Put music in the air;
And so it is at Christmastime,
We hear them everywhere.

The bells give forth a cheerful
    sound,
To lift our spirits high,
Ring out a message of good will,
That we cannot deny.

That Baby

Dolores Steger

Who is that baby there in the stall,
Sleeping so peacefully, tender and
    small?
Who is that baby, nodding right
    now,
As shepherds and wise men low to
    Him bow?
Who is that baby all praise at His
    birth?
That baby is Jesus, the Savior of
    earth.

When Angels Sang and Spoke

Cora M. Owen

Angels sang a joyful song,
When the night was very long,
To shepherds caring for their
    sheep.
Angels spoke with heavenly voice,
News that made their hearts
    rejoice,
That starry night on hillside steep.
    Jesus Christ is born!

The Holy Season

Nell Ford Hann

This is the holy season
To atune our hearts anew;
To the joy and peace of Christmas,
We especially wish for you.

It's time for love and laughter,
To permeate our home,
And to linger the whole year
    through,
After Christmas Day is gone.

Just Like My Baby Brother

Margaret Primrose

My baby brother can't play with a
   truck;
He can't roll a ball nor quack like
   a duck.
He's still too little to climb the
   stairs
And doesn't know how to say his
   prayers.

But Mom says Jesus was like that,
   too—
Too little to sing; too little to coo.
Yet He is the One who came to be
The very best friend of children
   like me.

Angelic Greeting

Sharon K. Kiesel

I'm a little angel—My daddy says
   that's right,
But that's not why I'm dressed
   like this, or standing here
   tonight.
This is the time we celebrate, the
   day of Jesus' birth,
And of the time when angels came
   with words of peace on earth.
Tonight we honor God on high
   with everything we do,
So now we start and I'm to say—
   Welcome to all of you!

This Joy

Cora M. Owen

I can't conceal
The joy I feel,
When Christmastime is near;
But this I know,
It's really so.
This joy can last all year.

The joy I feel—
This joy is real!
For Jesus came, you see,
From God above
To show His love.
My Savior God is He!

They Came to Bethlehem

Cora M. Owen

Riding on a lowly donkey,
   Mary came to Bethlehem,
Finding at the end of journey,
   That there was no room for
   them.

So they came unto the stable,
   Where her little Babe was born;
Laid Him in a hay-filled manger,
   Humble birthplace, not forlorn.

Shepherds came from fields to
   worship.
   Angels sang a holy song.
Star shone brightly in the heavens.
   Praises rang the whole night
   long.

One and Only

Carolyn R. Scheidies

Another year of Christmas cheer,
  Smiles painted on each face,
But forgotten in the rush
  Is the Savior's saving grace.

For Christmas is more than pre-
  sents,
  It's the coming of the one,
Who brings true joy to each
  human heart,
  Christ Jesus . . . God's one and
  only Son.
Song: "Silent Night! Holy Night!"
  (Optional: "O Holy Night")

Counting

Margaret Primrose

One, two, three.
I'm as glad as I can be
To tell you of Jesus' birth.

Four, five, six.
Let happy voices mix
For a Savior came to earth.

Seven, eight, nine.
I'm glad that He is mine,
And His promises are true.

I've only counted to ten,
But He died for millions of men
Because He loves them, too.

God's Greatest Gift

Margaret Primrose

The stable had no carpet,
  No holly on the door,
No strings of glowing lights,
  No games and toys galore.

There were no ribboned gifts
  Beneath a Christmas tree,
No stacks of greeting cards
  Addressed to you and me.

But this is where God gave
  The greatest gift of all,
Because the gift was Jesus,
  The Baby in the stall.

A Birthday Reminder

Nell Ford Hann

Poinsettias, evergreens and holly,
  Are beautiful reminders to me;
It is time to unpack the decora-
  tions,
And go in search for that perfect
  tree.

Poinsettias, evergreens and holly,
  In Christmas shades of green and
  red;
Remind us Jesus Christ, Our Lord
  and Savior
Has a birthday only—*(fill in)* days
  ahead.

Full of Questions

Margaret Primrose

Sometimes I'm full of questions
That start with how or when
Or where or who or what.
They seem to have no end.

But I never have to ask
Why Jesus was born in a stall.
He came to be our Savior
Because He loves us all.

The King in a Manger

Cora M. Owen

It was the King of kings
Who came to earth one day;
A tiny little Babe,
Who lay upon the hay.

It was the King of Heaven,
Born in a cattle stall.
In lowly manger bed,
They placed the Lord of all.

I Wish I Could Have Seen Him

Cora M. Owen

I wish I could have seen Him,
That little baby Boy,
That Precious One from Heaven,
Who came to bring us joy.

I wish I could have seen Him,
In manger where He lay;
The precious baby Jesus,
Upon His bed of hay.

The Christmas Fireplace

Nell Ford Hann

Our stockings are hung,
The holly . . . all strung,
  Flickering fire . . . the first of the
  season;
Christmas bells are ringing,
Caroling voices are singing,
  Jesus' birthday . . . that is the
  reason!

Peace Begins

Nell Ford Hann

Chaos ends . . . peace begins,
  In our hearts so deep within;
When we know the Prince of
  Peace,
  JESUS, our best friend.
Peace begins in each one's heart,
  God knew this was true;
That's why He sent the Prince of
  Peace,
  On Christmas Day for you!

One Message

Kimberly Seevers

One holy night
So very long ago
One holy baby
Born here below.
One simple message
For all the world to hear
Jesus brought redemption
For sinners everywhere.

10

Difficult

Wonderful Star

Cora M. Owen

(To be recited while looking at a star.)

Oh, glorious star!
You once led wise men on
To find the Holy Child.
By your light they were drawn.

Oh, wonderful star!
Send down your radiant light,
And show us all the way,
Unto the Christ tonight.

Christmas Sharing

Cora M. Owen

Christmas is a time to share,
What God has given you.
Others round you have a need,
And they need Jesus too.

Christmas is a time to give,
Expecting no return;
So give of self and what you
have.
Show others your concern.

God has given you His best,
When He sent forth His Son.
Share the news of Jesus' love.
It is for everyone.

Gifts

Dolores Steger

The Baby in the manger lay,
As prophesy foretold;
They brought to Him their pre-
sents rare,
Myrrh, frankincense and gold,
And, in return, He gave His gifts;
More precious you'll not find;
His gifts of hope and joy and
peace
He brought to all mankind.

We Have Gifts for You, Baby

Dolores Steger

We have gifts for You, Baby,
We have gifts for You, Son,
We have treasures of the ages,
Rightly Yours, Little One!

It's Your birthday, sweetest Man-
child,
It's Your birthday, Lamb so
dear,
It's Your wonder that we honor
With the presents we bring
here!

On this day of celebration,
On this day we've come from
far,
On this day we recognize You
And the miracle You are!

Imagine

Cora M. Owen

Imagine how it must have been,
To be a lowly shepherd when
The angels came upon their sight.
The sky was filled with heavenly
    light.

Imagine all the sudden fear,
When angels' words fell on their
    ear.
Imagine how they felt alarm,
And wondered if they would know
    harm.

Imagine now their great surprise,
When angels spoke from out the
    skies,
And try to feel their deepest joy,
When learning of the Baby Boy.

Imagine how they hurried there
And found the newborn Christ so
    fair;
Then think of how they went to
    tell,
The coming of Emmanuel.

Where Can I Find Him?

Kay Hoffman

It's hard to find the Christ Child
    It seems He's hid from view;
In all that we call Christmas
    It's hard to find a clue.

The shops are filled with finery,
    The world is tinsel bright—
Where is the humble stable place
    The Christ Child lay that night?

It's hard to hear the angel's song
    Above the world's loud din;
There're parties gay all over
    town,
    But do they honor Him?

Oh, tell me sage of ages past
    Where can I find the Child?
It seems the Christmas that I view
    The modern man has styled.

Far from the crowded city streets
    I sought a place apart,
And when I humbly knelt to pray
    I found Him in my heart.

Uncounted Stars

Donna Colwell Rosser

Pine-scented memories
    come gently to me
Through mists of emotion.
    Lightly, do
Joys of the past mingle
    softly, here and now,
As, our hopes for the future,
    we renew . . .

May life be filled with happiness,
    your smiles; uncounted stars
That lend their light
    to brighten darkest sky.
May Christmas be a moment
    unsurpassed. May what we have
Remind us that we've a gift
    only Jesus could buy.

This Holy Night . . .

Kay Hoffman

Come let us go this Holy night
  To Bethlehem afar;
The faith within our hearts will be
  Our bright and guiding star.

We, too, now seek the tiny Babe
  To worship and adore
As in that hallowed stable place
  Where shepherds knelt before.

No royal gifts like Magi brought
  Have we to take along,
But in our hearts will softly ring
  The angels' Christmas song.

We'll leave behind the hurried
    pace
  Of Christmas man-made style
And in the quiet of our hearts
  We'll find the Holy Child.

At Bethlehem

Alyce Pickett

Long, long ago near Bethlehem
  Some shepherds watched their
    sheep
While Joseph and Mary at the inn
  Could find no place to sleep.

Later, these found a stable
  With manger-bed and hay;
Here Mary's newborn Baby . . .
  The little Christ-Child lay.

The shepherds heard glad tidings,
  Heard praise from angels bright,
Then went to find the Holy Babe
  And worship Him that night.

This happened many years ago
  To people far away;
But we still need to find our Lord
  And worship Him today.

Gift of Love

Lillian Robbins

Oh, what a glorious morning!
  When Christmas comes around,
Sunshine bright above us,
  Or snow upon the ground.

No matter what the weather,
  Whether it's hot or cold.
Joy rings out across the land,
  With thrills like days of old.

We enjoy the celebration,
  To honor this special day.
Reminds us of love and blessings.
  "Merry Christmas," people say.

Through faith we know the Savior,
  And we thank the Lord above,
His gift surpasses everything.
  Jesus came to us in love.

Very Special

Cora M. Owen

God made a very special star,
To shine up in the sky,
To guide some wise men on their
way.
They knew Christ's birth was
nigh.

God made a very special choir,
To sing of Jesus' birth.
"Glory to God," was what they
sang,
"And peace to all the earth."

God made a very special place,
Where Jesus Christ was born;
And shepherds came and
worshiped there,
On that first Christmas morn.

God sent His very special Son,
To bring salvation down.
Because He loved us all so much,
He came to David's town.

Finding Jesus

Alyce Pickett

When God sent Jesus down to
earth
Bright angels robed in white
Told shepherds outside
Bethlehem
The wondrous news that night.

The happy men sang praises,
And hurried right away
To find the lowly manger-bed
Where little Jesus lay.

Magi, searching for the Lord,
Were shown a special star
To lead them into Bethlehem
From eastern lands afar.

The shepherds and the Magi
found
The Lord in Bethlehem;
Today we keep within our hearts
A dwelling place for Him.

Ring a Bell

Dolores Steger

Ring a bell for angels,
Announcing Jesus' birth,
Telling all the world below
He brings it peace on earth.

Ring a bell for shepherds
Who found the Baby small
Lying in a manger bed;
They spread the word to all.

Ring a bell for wise men
Who traveled from afar
With gifts of gold and incense,
Believing in a star.

Ring a bell for Christmas,
The birthday of God's Son
Who came as love forever,
And hope for everyone.

The Wise (?) Men

Vera Rush Hill

Alas! The star of Bethlehem
  Hangs atop the tree,
Placed there during Christmas
  For every eye to see.

But man forgets so quickly
  The purpose of the star—
A guiding light for wise men
  From near and yet so far.

Are we really "wise men"
  As we hang the star each year?
Or do we miss the meaning?
  Perhaps we've lost all fear?

Do we seek the manger
  As we look upon the star,
Or have we lost the purpose
  As our lives stay all ajar?

God used the star to teach us
  If we will only learn.
"Wise men" pause at Christmas,
  Its meaning to discern.

Christmas Lights

Vera Rush Hill

Are we caught up in the sparkle
  Of the lights upon the tree
Or do we see the message
  In its simplicity?

How Christ was sent to earth
  As the glowing Son Divine
To light the world at Christmas
  For needful humankind.

As we decorate the tree
  And plug in the final strings
Do we stand in awe of Christmas
  And the love of God it brings?

The warmth of Christmas lights
  And the beauty of the tree
Speak to all this season
  If man will hear and see!

Why Jesus Came

Alyce Pickett

If all the people in the world
  Today could only know
Why Jesus came from Heaven to
  us
  As a baby long ago;
Could know the love He felt for
  all
  Who lived on earth that day,
And know He still loves each of us
  In the same special way. . . .

Then we would study how to live
  As He wants us to do,
To be unselfish and be kind,
  Love and help others, too.
God's love would fill all of our
  hearts
  And what a change we'd see!
No one would fight, or hurt, or
  kill . . .
  Think how nice that would be!

Let's plant the thought within our
  hearts
  And help others to sow
This love for Jesus in their lives,
  So all the world can know.

One Christmas Eve

Alyce Pickett

A million stars that Christmas Eve
Shone brightly in the sky
While hillside shepherds watched
    in awe
Bright angels drawing nigh.

Angels that brought the glad
    tidings
About a Savior's birth . . .
God's only Son, Christ Jesus
That night had come to earth.

Let's listen on this Christmas Eve
As wondrous praises ring
In memory of that special gift,
The newborn Christ-Child King.

Come, sing along with mighty
    chorus
Who tell in thankful voice!
Our Savior came! Our Savior
    lives!
Give thanks, praise Him,
    Rejoice!

*Optional: Choir enters as last
stanza is read.*

All sing: "Joy to the World"

Come to Bethlehem

Margaret Primrose

*(May be sung to the tune of "Mary
Had a Little Lamb.")*

Come and go to Bethlehem,
    Bethlehem, Bethlehem.
Come and go to Bethlehem
    To see where Jesus slept.

Come and see the shepherds'
    fields,
Shepherds' fields, shepherds'
    fields.
Come and see the shepherds'
    fields
Where grazing flocks were
    kept.

Come and sing as angels sang,
    Angels sang, angels sang.
Come and sing as angels sang
    Announcing Jesus' birth.

Come and sway as camels swayed,
    Camels swayed, camels swayed.
Come and sway as camels swayed
    With wise men on their backs.

Follow them to find the King,
    Find the King, find the King.
Follow them to find the King
    And worship at His feet.

Heaven Sent

Nell Ford Hann

Let me tell you about the One,
  Who had a candle so bright,
That guided three wise men,
  Through the darkened night.
Birthday gifts laid at His feet,
  Were precious to behold,
Frankincense . . . myrrh
  And bright yellow gold.
The wise men and shepherds
  Gathered 'round, on knees bent,
They knew the babe in the
    manger,
For all . . . was Heaven-sent.
He's the Truth and the Light,
  His miracles never cease,
He's Jesus Christ, Son of God,
  Our blessed Prince of Peace.

God's Heavenly Gift

Nell Ford Hann

There's beauty in
  The season of Christmas,
With each cherished friend
  You meet;
There's a spirit of love
  At Christmas,
That's exchanged with each person
  You greet.

There's joy in the air
  In this season,
As we celebrate
  Lord Jesus' birth;
And proclaim to the world,
  God's heavenly gift,
Was sending His Son
  To earth!

Count Down

Nell Ford Hann

As we count down
  "Shopping days 'til Christmas"
Count each day as a special gift,
  That's one reason we honor
  Jesus,
He gives to our hearts,
  Love . . . with a lift!

As we count down
  "Shopping days 'til Christmas"
Accept each one His gift,
    wrapped for you;
  And how you unopen it,
Should be grateful
  And precious, too.

Christ in You

Nell Ford Hann

It does one proud,
  It makes one happy,
    When we do a worthy deed;
When we reach out,
  In compassion,
    To a brother that's in need.

It does one good,
  To help another,
    When they don't expect you
    to;
At Christmas . . . as
  Folks rise to the occasion,
    May they all see Christ in
    you!

When Jesus Came

Margaret Primrose

Sleeping at his mother's side,
  The tiniest lamb lay cuddled
Till a bright light shone and he heard a voice.
  Then he jumped to his feet—befuddled.

I think he saw the shepherds' fright
  But didn't know what it meant
When an angel spoke of the glory of God
  And a Babe that was heaven-sent.

I'm glad you and I, our family and friends
  Who know of the Savior's birth
Can join with the shepherds in thanking the Lord
  For the day Jesus came to earth.

Too Busy

Dixie Phillips

Middler age girl dressed like her mother; arms filled with packages.

Mother *(exhausted)*: I'm too busy shopping,
  I have no time for stopping
  To discover the true meaning of Christmas.
  Why—there's so much to do
  And by the time I'm through—
  I still don't know the true meaning of Christmas.
  There's cooking, cleaning and work galore!
  (Hands on hips.) I could mention a whole lot more!
  (Pause—cup ear.) What's that you say?
  Who came to take my sins away????
  (Point to manger.) This tiny Baby lying on the hay?
  (Looks thoughtfully in manger.)
  Oh! I've been much to busy to see.
  This Baby was born for me. *(Kneel beside manger.)*
  Come to my heart Lord Jesus—
  There's room in my heart for You!

Ready to Receive Him?

Cora M. Owen

They weren't ready to receive Him
In Bethlehem one day.
They weren't ready to believe Him
So they turned the Lord away.

Folks aren't ready to receive Him,
As He stands at the heart's door.
Folks aren't ready to believe Him.
He is turned away once more.

Are you ready to receive Him?
As we celebrate His birth?
Are you ready to believe Him,
God's own Son who came to earth?

Once Again

Dixie Phillips

Once again it's Christmas morning and happy church bells ring,
Children are dressed in their Sunday best, they begin to sing,
"Happy Birthday Jesus!" Their voices sweet and clear,
Rise up to the heavens to their precious Lord so dear.
It's not just another Christmas as His presence fills each heart,
Why, they sense "God is with us" right from the start.
No longer a Baby with a manger for His bed,
He's our living Savior, risen from the dead!
His presence that filled that stable the first Christmas night,
Fills the hearts of men and women with such great delight!
So, don't feel bad that you weren't there to present a gift of gold,
Because "His" Christmas story never will grow old.
He's still accepting gifts from wise men you see,
I'm planning to give Him a special gift just from me!
My gift can't be wrapped with a fancy bow,
You can't buy it at some fancy store, you know!
I'll tell you plain and simple right from the start,
The gift I plan to give to Him is all of my heart!
(Child holds up paper heart.)

Exercises

Let Him In

Carolyn R. Scheidies

Two groups

Narrator: Isaiah 9:6a

#1: In the darkness shone a light,
  Proclaiming the birth of a special child,
  Born in a Bethlehem night,
  Baby born to set our hearts to the right.

Song: "Angels We Have Heard on High" *(verses one and two)*

#2: For the tiny baby in that dusty stall,
  Was heralded by angel choir,
  Visited by shepherds who heeded the call,
  To worship the Lord of all.

Song: "Angels We Have Heard on High" *(verse three)*

All: Savior, King, we too come to Him,
  To the Christ born that long ago eve,
  The one who came to forgive sin.
  Lord, we kneel, to let you in. *(Kneel. Then stand to sing.)*

Song: "Angels We Have Heard on High" *(verse four)*

Special Bags

Helen Kitchell Evans

(All the children carry lovely shiny Christmas bags.)

Child 1: My little bag is filled with love.

Child 2: My bag holds blessings from above.

Child 3: My bag is filled with Christmas peace.

Child 4: My bag holds joy that will never cease.

Child 5: Here's a bag full of cheer.

Child 6: Mine is full of greetings for this time of year.

All: Special bags filled to give Happiness wherever you live.

Happy Birthday, Jesus

Alyce Pickett

Child 1
If Jesus had been born today,
Right now I'd be on my way
To find the stable where He lay.

Child 2
When I found the baby new,
I'd pat His hand and kiss Him, too.
I'd sing to Him, wouldn't you?

Child 3
That was a long time ago,
But I still love Jesus, so
I'll say it now and let Him know.

All
We love You, Jesus,
Happy birthday!

Big Bells, Little Bells

Margaret Primrose

First Child *(who holds a small bell):* Little bells.

Second Child *(with big bells):* Big bells.

Both Children: Listen to what they say.

First Child: Ding, ding, *(Rings the bell.)*

Second Child: Dong, dong. *(Rings the bell.)*

Both Children: Rejoice, it's Christmas Day! *(Both ring their bells.)*

First Child: Little bells, *(Rings bell.)*

Second Child: Big bells *(Rings bell.)*

Both Children: Ringing all day long
Ding dong, ding dong.
What a happy song!

(Could be done by one child with two bells.)

Children's Exercise and Song

Alyce Pickett

Doll in cradle at side of stage.
Five small children enter.

Child 1 *(sadly)*
I wish I had a gift to bring . . .
Something for the little King.

Child 2
I have no perfume, spice, or gold;
Just a blanket, if He gets cold.
    (Takes it to cradle.)

Child 3
This pretty rattle is a thing
You can shake *(Shakes.)* and make
    it ring.*(Puts it in cradle.)*

Child 4
I brought for baby Jesus sweet,
Little shoes for tiny feet. *(Puts*
    them in cradle.)

Child 5
My music box I think will be
Fun for Him; it was for me.
    (Places it in cradle.)

Child 1
I have no gift. What can I do?
    (Goes to cradle.)
Jesus, I give my love to You.

Offstage *(loudly):* The greatest
    gift is love.

All
For the little Christ-child king
The gift of love we all bring.

(Children sing to tune "Jesus
Loves the Little Children.")

Love Him, love Him, little
    children,
Love the precious One who came.
Love the One that angels bright
sang about that Christmas night;
Join their joyous songs of praise
to His dear Name.

Praise Him, praise Him, little
    children;
Praise the little Lord who came.
All our love to Him we bring
little Jesus Christ, the King
and we'll sing our songs of praise
to His dear Name.

It's Jesus' Birthday

Iris Gray Dowling

One Student
Lot's of people ask the question,
    What is Christmas all about?
It's time to celebrate the birthday
    of Jesus,
These Bible verses bring this
    out.

(Opens Bible and holds open as
class recites Luke 2:11, 12.)

Entire Class: "For unto you is
    born this day in the city of
    David a Savior, which is Christ
    the Lord. And this shall be a
    sign unto you; Ye shall find the
    babe wrapped in swaddling
    clothes, lying in a manger."

Bethlehem's Hill

Alyce Pickett

Child 1
Angel voices on Bethlehem's hill
Brought glad tidings of good
will.

Child 2
God had sent angels below
So we would be sure to know
About the little Savior's birth;
His only Son had come to earth.

Child 3
"You'll find the king," angels
said,
"In lowly stable manger bed."
Then shepherd men hurried away
To find the little Lord that day.

Child 1
Now, we can find the Savior, too.
He lives today for me and
(Points.) you, and you.

Who

Dolores Steger

Child 1: Who brings love on
Christmas morn
To a weary world and torn?

All: Jesus, Christ, the Lord.

Child 2: Who brings hope that
strife will cease
And that man will live in peace?

All: Jesus, Christ, the Lord.

Child 3: Who brings cleansing
from all sin,
So our hearts know joy within?

All: Jesus, Christ, the Lord.

Child 4: Who brings us eternity
That evermore with Him we'll
be?

All: Jesus, Christ, the Lord.
For these gifts, in one accord,
Shout for Jesus, Christ, the Lord;
Praise for Jesus, Christ, the Lord.

The Shepherds

Iris Gray Dowling

(Each child holds a picture in this order: shepherds with angel in sky; many angels in sky; and shepherds at manger.)

Child 1
The lowly shepherds trembled
When the angel appeared on
wing.

Child 2
The fearful men rejoiced
When they heard the messengers
sing.

Child 3
They rushed to Bethlehem's
manger
To find and worship the newborn
king.

23

The Shepherds' Response

Carolyn R. Scheidies

For a choir in background dressed as angels, actors in appropriate costumes pantomiming scenes, one or more narrators.

(Shepherds huddle around fire as narrator(s) speak.)

Narrator: On a night dark and cold,
Shepherds huddled around their fire,
When suddenly the sky was filled,
With a bright angel choir.

Song: "Angels, from the Realms of Glory" *(verses one and two)*

(Shepherds stare up in fear. An angel steps forward.)

Narrator: In fear the shepherd shook,
But an angel called, "Fear not. Behold
We bring you good news of the Messiah,
A promise kept of old." *(Steps back.)*

Angel Choir *(speak in unison):* A baby wrapped in swaddling clothes,
Is Jesus Christ the Lord,
Who lies now in Bethlehem,
In the stall where He was born.

Song: "Angels, from the Realms of Glory" *(verse three)*

(Narrator speaks as shepherds go to worship the baby Jesus.)

Narrator: Then the shepherds hurried
To the manger stall,
Went to kneel before the baby
Who was the king of all.

Song: "Angels, fom the Realms of Glory" *(last verse, refrain twice)*

A Shepherd's Point Of View

Carolyn R. Scheidies

Dress as shepherd, hold staff.

Come on. Come on.
There's something wonderful going on.
The Son of God was born tonight.
For as we shepherds huddled about our fire in the chill of the night,
(Keeping an eye on the sheep, of course.)
Overhead shown a bright light,
As we cowered in fear, an angel appeared.
"Fear not," said the angel, "for I bring good news to you."
"Christ the Lord is born this day in Bethlehem.
Go and you will find Him,
A baby lying in a manger stall. The Savior of us all."
Then, suddenly, the whole sky exploded into song
As an angel choir sang along.
Sang to us, poor lowly shepherds spending the night in the chill.
I mean, even the local rabbi passes on the other side of the hill . . .
When we come on the scene.
We don't smell the best, you see . . . out all day with the sheep.
Our great King David may have been a shepherd boy in his day,
But these days we don't aspire so high.
We've learned to keep our own company,
Forgotten by most of the folks,
Ignored by the rest . . . until tonight.
Don't you see what this means?
God hasn't forgotten us!
God himself cared enough to tell us about the birth,
The Messiah come to earth.
And you ask me, am I going to see HIM!
If God cares enough about shepherds to tell us about His Son,
I want to see Him, this One.
I MUST see Him, God's only Son.
Come on. Come on.
Come follow me to the stable stall,
As I go to worship the newborn King, the Savior of us all.

Song: "Thou Didst Leave Thy Throne"

Go, Tell It on the Mountains

Ingrid Shelton

A Christmas play for nine primary/junior students.

Characters: Narrator, three shepherds, Mary, Joseph, Baby Jesus, woman, young man, old man

Props: a creche with Baby Jesus and a star above, three doors *(front of houses)*

Music: "Silent Night! Holy Night!" *(one verse)*

Narrator *(reads)*: Luke 2:8-14

(Three shepherds are walking toward the creche.)

First Shepherd:	The angel told us It's not very far We'll find the baby Under that star. *(Points to the star.)*
Second Shepherd:	"The Savior is born." The angel said That's the biggest miracle I've heard of yet.
Third Shepherd:	What wonderful news In Bethlehem here Let's worship Him Our Savior, so dear.

Music: "Silent Night! Holy Night!" *(one verse)*

(Shepherds kneel in front of crib.)

Narrator *(reads):* Luke 2:17

(Shepherds get up and begin walking toward doors.)

First Shepherd:	Let's quickly go And tell young and old God sent us the Savior As the prophets foretold.
Second Shepherd:	It amazes me How God loves me To give me life Eternally.

Third Shepherd *(excited, knocks at the first door, a woman appears)*:
Our Savior was born!
A few doors away
We've just seen Him
Come, worship, and pray.

Woman *(rubs her eyes):* I'm busy right now
And tired, too
Don't bother me, Shepherd
Who knows if it's true.

First Shepherd *(excited, knocks at the second door, a young man appears):* Wake up! Get up!
Good news for all
Our King is born
In Bethlehem's stall.

Young man *(stares at the shepherd for a moment):*
What? Are you crazy?
A king in a stall?
Beat it! Get lost!
Or I'll punch you all.
(He shakes a fist at the shepherds.)

Second Shepherd: Oh, it's so sad
They refuse to believe
Our Savior and Lord
They won't receive.

Third Shepherd *(knocks at the third door, an old man appears):*
Sir, a miracle!
Born this night
Was Christ, our Savior
Under that starlight. *(Points to it.)*

Old Man: You're sure it happened?
(The three shepherds nod their heads.)
Then glory to God
I'm coming to worship
My Savior! My Lord!

Music: "Oh, Come, Let Us Adore Him" *(one verse)*
(The old man follows the three shepherds to the creche. They all kneel in front of it.)

Narrator: Will you receive Jesus
Your Savior today
He was born to save you
Come, worship, and pray.*(Reads John 1:12)*

The Gifts of Christmas

Karen H. Whiting

This program is part of an evening of caroling. Each gift is opened and explained then followed by a Christmas carol.

Cast: Narrator, Seven Gift Bearers, Angel holding a baby, Mary and Joseph

Gifts: candle, wreath, candy cane, angel, star, and dove are gift wrapped. One gift contains a paper with message telling us to "look around."

Seven children enter holding wrapped packages and place them on stage.

Narrator: Christmas is a time of joy, a time of peace. Christmas is a time when families gather and exchange gifts. God is the greatest gift giver. The packages here today will remind us of God's gifts to us.

Song: "O Little Town of Bethlehem"

Child 1: Our first gift opened is a candle. The candle gives light. On that silent night long ago, God gave us light. Jesus, the light of the world, gives His light to us. We can help bring light to the world when the light of Jesus shines in us.

Song: "Silent Night! Holy Night!"

Child 2: The second gift opened is a wreath. The wreath, made of evergreens, is in the shape of a circle. This gift reminds us of eternal life. God's love is eternal. Like the circle, God's love has no ending. When we give love, we discover it circles back to us.

Song: "Love of the Ages" or "Love Divine, All Love Excelling!"

Child 3: This candy cane is the third gift opened. The red of love and white of purity are entwined together in the shape of a shepherd's staff. Shepherds were the first to come worship Jesus. Jesus, the Good Shepherd, cares for us as a shepherd cares for his sheep. Let us worship Jesus and accept God's loving care.

Song: "Away in a Manger"

Child 4: Gift number four is an angel. This is a gift of joy. The angels proclaimed the news of Jesus' birth and sang out praising God. We too, can be messengers and sing out joyfully, proclaiming the meaning of Christmas to others.

28

Song: "Go, Tell It on the Mountain"

Child 5: The fifth gift opened is a dove. This is a gift of peace. At Christ's birth, angels proclaimed, "Peace on earth to men of good will." It is in being gentle, like a dove, that we help bring peace on earth.

Song: "God Rest Ye Christian Gentlemen"

Child 6: The sixth gift opened is a star. The star shone above for all to see yet only a few followed it. The star guided the wise men to Jesus, the newborn King. Jesus desires to be the star in your life, guiding you to the Father. Be wise and choose to follow Him.

Song: "We Three Kings"

Child 7: The seventh gift contains a message telling us to look around and see what God has given us. *(Child points to side stage and Mary and Joseph enter.)* Behold Mary and Joseph. God gave Jesus a family. Their start, in a stable, was humble, but the important thing was their unity and love for one another. We help our family be united by our love and acceptance of the family God gave us.

Song: "O, Mary Did You Know?"

Angel *(enters holding a baby):* The reason for Christmas is seen in the last and most precious gift—it cannot be contained in a package—the Christ Child. When we see a baby we marvel at the gift of life. God gave us His only Son that whoever believes in Him might have everlasting life.

Song: "What Child Is This?"

Christmas Program

V. Louise Cunningham

Cast:
Shepherds: Mitch, Brad, John
Angels: Sarah, Cheri, Josie
Wise Men: Justin, Matt, Aaron
Nativity Group: Steve, Joseph; Kelsey, Mary; Kevin, Innkeeper
Pastor Reed: ~~Youth Pastor~~ *Youth Coordinator*

Setting: A youth meeting in a fellowship hall and outside the door

Props: Basketball, chairs

Scene One

Mitch and Justin aside from the meeting place.

Mitch: Let's go shoot some hoops.
Justin: I can't.
Mitch: Sure you can, I know you don't have homework tonight.
Justin: I can't. There's something else.
Mitch: You didn't sign up to be in that Christmas play at church.—You did. I can tell by your face. You're in it because of Kelsey.
Justin: That's not the only reason. Pastor Reed needs more people for speaking parts. He could use you.
Mitch: No way. I'm not dressing up in a bathrobe.
Justin: They don't dress in bathrobes. Sarah will be there.
Mitch: Well, maybe I'll go and watch you.

Scene Two

Youth gathered in Fellowship Hall.

Pastor Reed: I want you to break up into groups by characters, angels, wise men, and shepherds and the nativity group. That includes Joseph, Mary, and the innkeeper. Imagine what it would be like to be an angel, shepherd or a wise man during the time of Jesus. What was it like for Mary to be pregnant without a husband? How did Joseph feel or the innkeeper? Okay, let's do it. I'm glad to see you, Mitch. I need another shepherd so if you'd go with that group.
Mitch: I'm just kind of here to watch Justin.

Pastor Reed: Well, he's a wise man. You can go with him, but I could really use you with the shepherds, if you don't mind sitting in with them.

Mitch: Okay, but I'm just watching.

(Group divides. Lights focus on the group speaking. There is a lot of laughing going on as they think of angel names.)

Sarah: This script is really dumb. It calls for angels by numbers. Angel one, Angel two.

Cheri: It would be easy to make up names for angels, one could be called Celestial.

Sarah: How about Astral or Galaxy?

Cheri: There could be Cosmos, Universe or Solar.

Josie: There were two angels named in the Bible, Michael and Gabriel.

Sarah: True, but I like Celestial and Galaxy the best. I think they're heavenly.

Josie: Pastor Reed just looked at us, I guess we'd better get to the questions.

Cheri: So what's the question?

Josie: What would it have been like to be an angel in Heaven waiting for Jesus to be born?

Sarah: What do angels do besides worship God?

Cheri: I think they sit around blowing up clouds

(All laugh.)

Josie: I think Michael called a meeting of all the angels to tell them God was going to save people from their sins by sending Jesus to earth as a baby.

Sarah: In that meeting, I suppose they found out who would go tell the shepherds.

Cheri: I wonder how they decided that?

Sarah: They could have drawn straws.

Cheri: That doesn't sound very biblical.

Josie: Sounds as good as casting lots. They did that a lot in the Old Testament and even in the New Testament.

Sarah: What if they drew names and made it like an awards ceremony. You know, they open the golden envelope and the names of the lucky ones are read out.

Josie: Okay. Let's say all the angels want to go to Bethlehem. They go to the meeting and Michael is the MC. Gabriel holds the golden envelope.

Cheri: I think Michael would take time to explain why it had to be Bethlehem and then he'd read the names.

Sarah: After that, the lucky angels would have practice sessions learning to speak together, "I bring you good news of great joy that will be for all people."

Josie: That answers the next question. The attitude of the angels would be one of great excitement, right?

Sarah: What would the other angels do?

Cheri: I think they floated on clouds around Bethlehem watching.

(Lights fade on Angel group and center on the Shepherds.)

Mitch: Do shepherds have to wear bathrobes? I'm just curious.

Pastor Reed: No. They have regular costumes to wear.

Mitch: That's a relief. Of course I didn't say I'd do it.

(Shepherds all laugh.)

Brad: We wear scarfs on our heads.

John: That's better than a turban like the wise man.

(Shepherds nod agreement.)

Mitch: Sure it is.

Pastor Reed: Matter of fact, I think we have time today to see what costumes are available. Now we'd better get to the questions. When you think about the attitudes of the shepherds, also discuss what they did after the angels left. Remember shepherds were almost the outcasts of that society. *(Exits group.)*

Brad: I think the shepherds were sort of like teenagers.

John: Why do you say that?

Mitch: Don't tell me you've never had adults treat you like you are really weird.

John: That's true—but you really are weird!

Mitch: No worse than you.

Brad: I think the shepherds were men who liked animals and enjoyed spending a lot of time outside.

John: I picture them all sitting around a campfire when the angels came. Imagine what a shock that would be to look up and see all those angels. I'd be scared.

Mitch: I wonder if each one thought they were dreaming and no one else saw it.

John: I bet they'd be ~~exited~~ excited, too. They'd been waiting for a Messiah for a long time.

Brad: They believed, because as soon as the angels left, the shepherds went to find the baby Jesus.

John: Then they went around telling everyone.

Mitch: If they were outcasts, a lot of people wouldn't pay much attention to them.

Brad: It's hard to be excited about something and then not have anybody care or listen to what you have to say.

John: At least they had the satisfaction of obeying God.

Mitch: If I had angels coming to me, I'd do what they said.

Brad: Is that any different than obeying God and doing what the Bible

32

says today?

Mitch: Not really. This is getting pretty deep.

John: That's what we're supposed to do.

Brad: Our answer is, the shepherds were scared but excited.

John: I think these questions are designed to help us portray the shepherds well in the play.

Brad: I'm sure that's the plan.

(Lights fade on Shepherds then center on Wise men group.)

Justin: We're going to figure out how the wise men might have felt at making the trip and seeing the baby Jesus. Except Jesus was a child by the time they got to see him. We shouldn't even be in the nativity picture.

Aaron: Maybe they'll explain that or we're in a different scene. I haven't seen the script.

Justin: Back to the wise men and their feelings.

Matt: They were rich to be able to take time off from work.

Aaron: Maybe they got a government grant for research. *(Laughs.)*

Matt: They had to be rich. They brought gifts of gold, frankincense and myrrh.

Aaron: Wonder how big their tents were.

Justin: They'd travel in a motor home instead of tents now.

Matt: It wouldn't have been too hard on them. If they were rich they wouldn't have to do any work setting up camp.

Aaron: True. They would sit around and have people wave feather fans to cool them off and wait for somebody to cook their dinner.

Justin: I wonder if they had young boys to take care of the camels?

Matt: They can be real mean.

Aaron: Who the camel boys? *(Laughs.)*

Matt: No, the camels. They spit a long way too.

Justin: Those camel boys probably had to work all the time. I wonder if that made up for going on a long trip and seeing a lot of the world.

Aaron: I bet they missed their families.

Justin: Do you think they got to see Jesus?

Aaron: I think there would have been at least one of the wise men who would have seen to it that anyone who wanted to could have seen and worshiped Jesus.

Justin: They might have brought presents of their own.

(Lights fade on Wise Men then center on nativity group.)

Kelsey: We're to explain how our person might have felt. Who wants to start?

Kevin: I will. I think the innkeeper got a bad rap. He at least provided a place for Mary and Joseph to stay. He might have let his wife or a servant girl help.

Steve: That's possible. Mary and Joseph had probably been to other inns and they all must have had their "No Vacancy" signs up.

Kelsey: I keep wondering about Mary. During the time she lived, she could have been stoned to death for being pregnant and not married.

Steve: Have you stopped to think how many stonings there would be today for adultery or unwed mothers?

Kevin: There'd be lots! My grandma says that in her growing up days in the 50s if a girl got pregnant she usually went to visit relatives and the baby was adopted.

Steve: Was that the dark ages?

Kevin: Not quite. Today the first thought of our society is to have an abortion if you don't want a baby.

Kelsey: But Mary wouldn't do that even today. She was visited by an angel and she knew that she was going to carry the Son of God.

Steve: Why do you think she went to visit her cousin Elizabeth so soon afterwards?

Kelsey: She probably needed to talk to someone. She told Joseph she was going to have a baby. She knew from his reaction that he didn't believe her.

Steve: He did after the angel came and talked to him.

Kelsey: But until then, imagine what Mary felt.

Steve: Joseph wasn't happy either. I think he was hurt and probably felt Mary preferred someone younger.

Kevin: He cared enough about her to be willing to divorce her quietly before the angel came and explained things. He didn't want her involved in a scandal.

Kelsey: He showed love that way.

(Lights fade.)

Scene 3

Outside of the meeting place.

Justin: How was your practice?

Mitch: Not too bad.

Justin: I noticed Sarah's eyes lit up when she saw you come in. Saw you talking to her afterwards.

Mitch: Well, she was wondering if we could get together and practice our lines.

Justin: I knew it. I knew it. You're going to be in it. And you said what to practicing with her.

Mitch *(laughs):* I thought I could work it in.

Justin: How many lines do you have?

34

Mitch *(laughs):* About three. Our group got pretty deep thinking about what it was like for the shepherds. Did yours?

Justin: Ours did towards the end. It's another one of Pastor Reed's plans. He's always trying to make the Bible come alive by seeing Bible people as real people with problems like us.

Mitch: I could see some of the problems they'd have with the way they dressed. It's not easy tying one of those scarf things around your head. If it's too loose everything falls down in your eyes. If it's too tight it gives you a headache.

Justin: I bet Sarah could tie it just right!

Mitch: You're just jealous Kelsey didn't ask you to help her practice her lines.

Justin: How do you know she didn't? *(Smiles.)*

Mitch *(keeps repeating as they exit):* Did she? Well did she?

Christmas Bells

Beverly C. Bishop

This program is designed for presentation by a small class of six to seven year olds. They may each hold a bell and ring it when it's time for their part, or bells may be cut from poster board for each child to hold.

First Child: The Christmas bells ring clear and loud
For everyone to hear.
They tell the Christmas story
To all, both far and near.

Second Child: My bell tells of the angel throng
In earthly skies who sang their song.

Third Child: My bell tells of Jesus' birth;
The Son of God come down to earth.

Fourth Child: My bell tells that shepherds heard
And came to see them spread the Word.

Fifth Child: We ring our Christmas bells again,
We ring them now and pray
That God's own Son will come to live
Within your heart today.

(Option: The song "Gospel Bells" may be sung to conclude the presentation.)

If I Could Be a Christmas Card . . .

Judy Carlsen

This program is designed so all children can participate. Each part can easily be divided in order to accommodate more children. Or, it can be used by a youth group. Props are good to have, but not necessary. Special costumes are also optional.

Narrator: It's that time of year again—Christmas card and letter time. No doubt you have already received Christmas greetings from people you know well and from those you only hear from this season of the year. What type of cards have you received? Even more importantly, what kind are you sending? The kind of Christmas card you send says a lot about what you think of Christmas. Let's see what these friends can tell us about their choice of Christmas cards this year.

Scene 1—Fifth and Sixth Graders

1 *(wears party hat):* If I could be a Christmas card,
I'd be all shiny and bright.
My picture would show a festive time—
A party to last all night.

2 *(wears Santa hat and carries wrapped gift):* And don't forget old Santa,
That jolly man in red.
Who loves to give out gifts
To Stacy, Jack and Ted.

3 *(carries fake food or pictures of food):* Yes! Santa is the coolest—
He likes to bring us fun.
And Christmas is the best time
For food 'til day is done.

4 *(carries jar of nuts and box of chocolates):* Now, don't forget the goodies—
They're part of this great season:
Mints and chocolates by the box,
And nuts for any reason.

36

5 There is no doubt that Christmas
Is all of this and more—
Food, parties, decorations,
Santa, gifts galore!

Song: "Jingle Bell Rock" or "Have a Holly, Jolly Christmas"

Scene 2—Third and Fourth Graders

1 *(shows picture of fireplace and Christmas tree):* If I could be a
Christmas card,
My picture would look warm
With fireplace and Christmas tree,
And family all at home.

2 *(shows picture of children in pajamas opening gifts):*
The children in my picture
Would wear their red-striped jammies.
Their eyes are big as saucers
To see their gifts from Grammy.

3 *(shows picture of people singing around piano):* Then at the old piano
The clan would gather 'round
To sing their favorite carols.
Ah, love and joy abound!

4 *(carries a few decorations):* Christmas decorations
Add a homey, festive touch.
The wreath, lights and ribbons.
The candles glow so much!

5 And, so, my Christmas card,
With home and family,
Highlights love and warmth
That mean so much to me.

Song: "I'll Be Home for Christmas" or "The Christmas Song"

Scene 3—First and Second Graders

1 *(shows picture of cardinal and deer):* If I could be a Christmas card,
There'd be a lot of snow,
Some beautiful red cardinals,
A little fawn and doe.

2 *(dresses for outdoors or shows picture of children dressed that way):*
Children wearing snowsuits
Will zoom down hill on sled.
While others make their snowman
With a hat upon his head.

3 *(shows picture of sleigh):* Christmas means a sleigh ride,
With lots of friends aboard.
It's so much fun to glide on snow,
The cold air is ignored.

4 *(shows ice skates or picture of ice skates):* And what could be
more beautiful
Than ice skating at night?
The skaters make figure 8s,
The stars shine—what a sight!

5 Yes, Christmas is the highlight
Of winter, it is true—
The snow and ice, the frost, the stars,
And winter animals too.

Song: "Let It Snow," "Winter Wonderland" or "Frosty the Snowman"

Scene 4—Beginners and Kindergarteners

1 *(shows picture of Jesus):* If I could be a Christmas card,
I know what I would be.
I'd have a great big picture
Of the One who came for me.

2 *(shows picture of baby Jesus):* He's Jesus, God's own Son,
Who started out so small.
He came to earth from Heaven
As Savior of us all.

3 *(shows picture of the nativity):* My card would show Mary,
The stable and the cow,
The angels and the shepherds
Who before the Babe did bow.

4 *(shows picture of wise men):* Afar off are the wise men
Who traveled from afar,
Over hill and valley,
Following that star.

5 *(show picture of heart with words "Jesus loves you!"):*
Christmas is a lot of things
To people you might know.
But the most important thing is:
Jesus loves us so!

Song: "Jesus Loves Me"

Song: "Away in a Manger" *(with motions)*

Narrator: Christmas is more than fun, gifts,
More than love, family,
More than snow, beauty of nature.
Christmas is God's loving gift to people of sending His Son.

(All children sing closing songs.)

Song: *(Tune of "London Bridge")*
Christmas is God's gift of love *(3 times)*
Christ Our Savior.

Song: "O Come, Let Us Adore Him" *(4 verses)*

Thanksgiving

A Thankful Day

Iris Gray Dowling

Thanksgiving is a day of
  remembering,
A day to be thankful and joyful,
A day to spend time thinking what
  Jesus did
When He died and arose again.

Take Time

Iris Gray Dowling

Take time to be thankful
This coming Thanksgiving Day;
Sing praises and worship the
  Lord;
Tell Him your thanks as you
  pray.

Friends

Dolores Steger

Thank You, God, for listening
And answering my prayer
By giving me so many friends
Who show me that they care,
Friends that I can count on
When I need them; they'll be
  there.

Your Child

Dolores Steger

Thank You, God, for childhood,
And for making me,
And thanks for letting me just know
Your child I'll always be.

Large and Small

Carolyn R. Scheidies

Thank You Lord Jesus
For blessings large and small,
But, for always being near . . .
I *(we)* thank You most of all.

He Provides

Dolores Steger

God provides for our comfort,
Provides for our care;
Give praise on Thanksgiving;
Our Lord's always there.

Blessings From God

Dolores Steger

Turkey and stuffing
Really do rate,
But it's blessings from God
That make Thanksgiving great.

Forget Not

Cora M. Owen

When you are tempted to com-
    plain,
Just count your blessings once
    again;
And pay attention to each one.
You'll find your list is just begun.

Thank God for many worthwhile
    things.
Enjoyment from the Father
    springs.
Forget not every benefit,
That comes from God, the
    Infinite.

Thanksgiving Prayers

Nell Ford Hann

Thanksgiving prayers are not
    "leftovers",
  They are the main entree;
Nourishment to sustain soul and
    spirit,
  As home cooking to the body
    this holiday.
So the prayers I pray on
    Thanksgiving,
  Are original and . . . . . . true;
As I ask for God's many blessings,
  To rain, abundantly, down on
    you!

Blessings and Memories

Nell Ford Hann

Blessings and memories
  Are what we have today,
We are making memories
  That will never go away.

We are counting God's blessings,
  That are innumerable, it's true;
And may His love, grace and
    mercy,
  Abound, abundantly, on you!

I Bow My Head With
Great Thanksgiving

Nell Ford Hann

I bow my head with great
    Thanksgiving,
  I lift my hands in praise;
I worship You . . . O Worthy
    Master,
  On this November day.

I thank You for the many
    blessings,
  You have bestowed on me;
And all the joy that fills my heart,
  For homeland of brave and free.

I bow my head with great
    Thanksgiving,
  God . . . I ask of You in prayer;
At all the holiday banquet tables,
  They'll feel Your presence
    there.

God Is Good

Lillian Robbins

God is good, people say.
  He gives such perfect things.
It's not enough to just say thanks,
  But that is what I mean.

I love the beauty of all the earth.
  God made it's plains and hills,
The summer sun and winter snow,
  Each season brings me thrills.

Grown-ups say this land is great
  For people just like me.
It gives us freedom to work and
  play,
And worship, too, you see.

Other blessings God gives to us.
  We all should be quite pleased.
For all the things He gives to me,
  I thank Him on my knees.

Giving Thanks

Kay Hoffman

I never cease to marvel
  At the wonder of God's world.
Flowers, trees and songbirds
  And tiny leaves unfurled.

I lift my eyes to Heaven
  To skies so soft and blue,
And marvel how each day, our
  God,
  Sends His gifts anew.

The gentle rain, the summer sun,
  The harvest in the fall,
From out the fullness of the earth
  God blesses one and all.

In gratitude I bow my head
  And send a prayer above
Giving thanks for all His gifts
  And for His precious love.

We Couldn't Count Them

Cora M. Owen

If we should start to make a list
  Of all that God has done,
I'm sure we couldn't count them
  all,
Or name them everyone.

If we should start to count the
  ways,
  In which we have been blessed,
I'm sure we couldn't count them
  all.
  He gives us all His best.

Where to Start

Carolyn R. Scheidies

It's hard to count my (our)
  blessings,
  But I know just where to start.
I want to thank You, Jesus,
  For living in my (our) heart.
  Thank You Jesus!

I'm Thankful as Can Be

Helen Kitchell Evans

I'm just filled full of wishes
For this Thanksgiving Day
Thankful for my daddy
And for his weekly pay.

Thankful for my mother
And all she does for me,
And for the pretty clothes I wear
I'm thankful as can be.

We Give Thanks

Kay Hoffman

We thank Thee, Lord, for precious
    grain,
For the fruit upon the vine,
For festive bird and fam'ly
    gatherings
That mark Thanksgiving time.

We thank Thee, Lord, for this dear
    land
Where freedom rings for all;
For rivers wide and canyons deep,
    For mountains grand and tall!

Each season with its special joys
    Is a blessing from Thy hand,
And all the fullness of the earth
    Is by Thy goodness planned.

We lift our thanks this day, O
    Lord,
    As now we humbly pray;
But may our greater "thanks" be
    shown
In serving Thee each day.

A Special Day

Cora M. Owen

It's good to have a special day,
    In which to thank the Lord;
To realize what He has done.
    That must not be ignored.

But we don't need a special day,
    To bring our thanks to Him;
For we should thank Him **every**
    day,
    With hearts filled to the brim.

This Holiday . . . Thanksgiving

Nell Ford Hann

They call this Holiday . . .
    Thanksgiving,
    The whole reason, I believe,
Is to give "Thanks" to our Father
    God,
    For the blessings we receive.

We thank Him for our bountiful
    harvest,
    We thank Him for His
    unconditional love,
We thank Him for His abundant
    blessings,
    He showers down on us from
    above.

This year as we are "thanks" and
    "giving"
    When you bow your heads to
    pray,
Praise Him for "thanks" and
    "receiving"
For we're truly blessed today!

43

Not Just One Special Day

Helen Kitchell Evans

I give thanks today
For all God gives to me,
But when tomorrow comes
I'll be thankful, too, you see,
Because God cares for me
Each day throughout the year,
Not just on one special day
When Thanksgiving Day is here.

Let Them Know

Helen Kitchell Evans

Do we take advantage
Of an opportunity to say
"Thank you", or "you did well
I'm proud of you today?"

The child learning to swim
Is helped when given praise;
We can give our children hope
In many, many ways.

Does the mailman we see each
day
Walking through sleet and snow
Ever get a kind word?
Do you care? Well, let him
know.

Each new dawn is a gift from
God,
We can be selfish or we can
give,
But on this Thanksgiving and
every day
Let's love and help others to
live.

Gratitude

Alta McLain

My heart is filled with gratitude.
Some things are very dear.
Thanks for the flowers blooming,
Birds singing with good cheer.
For all the lovely things you give
I will praise You, Lord. I know
That beauty is a gift from God
To help us live and grow.

Thank You for Courage

Lillian Robbins

Thank You, Lord for courage
To face each new day.
Sometimes I am puzzled,
Don't know what to say.

I always look to Heaven,
Speak troubles just to You.
Your presence gives me comfort,
Will surely see me through.

I know You're there to guide me
And keep me on the track.
And when I sometimes falter,
You'll gently lead me back.

Alone I can do nothing;
Your love can make it sure.
You guide my steps to victory
And make my heart stay pure.

To You I'm always grateful,
My heart is filled with love,
I know that all my blessings.
Come from You, God up above.

Why Am I Thankful?

Lillian Robbins

May be presented by adults and children if desired.

Characters:
  Announcer
  Three Pilgrims
  Two Indians
  Housewife
  Patient (and attendant)
  Preacher
  Little Girl
  Teacher
  Mother
  Christian
  Sunday School Teacher
  Widow
  Boy
  Orphan
  Teen
  Grandmother
  Football Player

Costumes: Each child dressed appropriately to represent the character for which they speak.

Announcer: For what can we be thankful at a time like this? That question arises among social groups, religious groups, and in the hearts of individuals during this Thanksgiving season. Our lives are often so hectic, we hardly recognize the blessings which are ours. But tonight we are going to get a peep-hole view of the lives of individuals from different walks of life, and our minds will share some thoughts with them about Thanksgiving.

First, we will roll back the time to long ago in the early days of the settlers on American soil. When those travelers left their homeland far away, they could not possibly have known what lay ahead of them in the months to come.

Their concerns were somewhat different from ours. They didn't worry about getting off work at 5 o'clock to attend a party, or shopping

45

for a new car, or taking their children to the dentist or music lessons, or who would win the championship ball game.

They were anxious about how to stay warm, how to get food, how to treat physical ailments. In the darkness of the night and the heat of the summer sun, they must have meditated about the misfortunes and hardships they endured. But then came the time to rejoice in their blessings. Let's join some of those Pilgrims now.

(All three Pilgrims enter.)

First Pilgrim *(carrying ears of corn)*: The idea of Thanksgiving began from our experiences when we were new settlers in this wonderful place which became the homeland of our people.

Second Pilgrim *(carrying a pumpkin):* The voyage across the ocean was long and frightening. We landed here after many days and nights on the waters. The winter was cold. Our people suffered, and many of them died. But when spring came, some of the native Indians helped us plant seeds.

Third Pilgrim *(carrying a bag of beans):* Now harvest has been reaped and our hearts are filled with thanksgiving to the Lord for bringing us to this great land of freedom and for saving our lives through the hard times we've had.

First Pilgrim: We are so excited now. We are going to have a feast to celebrate our blessings, and our Indian friends will share with us.

(Two Indians enter—both carry wood for a fire.)

First Indian: It was strange to have these white men come to our shores. Their ways were different from our ways, but they needed shelter and food to survive.

Second Indian: We are thankful we were able to help them. Now we are going to share a celebration together because we can live here in peace. *(Pilgrims and Indians exit.)*

Announcer: Many years have passed since those days. Times have changed, crops are more plentiful, and we find ourselves a part of a prosperous nation. Tonight, there are some characters here who will bring us up to modern times and remind us of thoughts which many people share in today's society.

Housewife *(carrying candlestick or some other household item):* I'm a new housewife. And I am thankful the Lord let me meet such a wonderful young man. My husband and I are just beginning a new home, and we are thankful that the Lord has led the two of us to share our lives together in this very special way. *(Exits.)*

Patient *(carrying crochet yarn and needle—someone wheels her in):* This is my third year in this wheelchair. Some people feel sorry for me, but they just don't understand how much the Lord has blessed me. I don't have the use of my legs, but my mind is alert, and I can use my hands. And I am thankful my family and friends love me and help me. *(Exits.)*

Little Girl *(carrying doll):* I'm just a little girl. But I know many things to be thankful for. Most of all, I am thankful for my mom and dad. *(Exits.)*

Teacher *(carrying stack of books):* I am thankful to be able to do the one thing I always wanted to do, teach little children. There are many teachers like me who get up every morning determined to help our youth develop their potentials in every area of learning. It is not always easy, but it is very rewarding when students cooperate. *(Exits.)*

Mother *(carrying toy, item of clothing, or walking in with small child):* I feel like the mothers we read about in the Old Testament who felt that one of God's greatest blessings was to become a mother. I love my children dearly and thank the Lord for each one of them. *(Exits.)*

Christian *(carrying white Bible):* I'm a Christian. I thank God for parents and teachers who have taught me about God. And I thank Jesus for living and dying for me. *(Exits.)*

Sunday School Teacher: When little children come into my Sunday school class, I am just so thankful. As a Sunday school teacher, I get to know the sweet little girls and the rowdy little boys and to love every one of them. I thank God for letting me teach them about His love. *(Exits.)*

Widow *(carrying photo book):* God has been good to me. I had a wonderful husband for many years. Now I might be considered a lonely widow by some people, but I'm not really lonely. *(Opens photo book and looks at it.)* I have wonderful memories, loving friends, and a merciful Savior. I can only say, "Thank you, Lord." *(Exits.)*

Boy *(carrying skates or skate board):* I'm thankful for a good place to live and for plenty of good food to eat. It makes me grow strong so I can have lots of fun. And that's what I like—fun. *(Exits.)*

Orphan *(carrying stuffed dog or bear):* When my mom and dad died, my heart was broken. I was an orphan, and I was afraid. I'm not alone any more, and I'm thankful for people who love me and help me. *(Exits.)*

Preacher *(excited—carrying Bible):* Preachers like me enjoy this season. There is a lot of pleasure and fun in celebration, but there is a serious thought about the Lord's blessings, too. He has blessed us with the truth of His Word *(Holds up Bible.)* and the opportunity to spread the gospel. I thank Him for freedom to worship and to serve in every spot of our nation and to carry the message across the seas. *(Exits.)*

Teen *(carrying car keys):* Sometimes teens may appear to be unappreciative, but there are many young people like me who really feel thankful for all the good things in life. Yes, I'm even thankful for my parents, and my little sister, and my brother. I'm thankful for good friends, and for the Lord,—and of course my car is close to the top of my list of things to be thankful for. *(Shows keys to audience—exits.)*

Grandmother *(carrying picture of baby):* Many years have passed since I saw my little one begin the journey through life. I was so thrilled with that little baby, I could hardly imagine anything else so wonderful. But now I'm a grandmother, and I thank the Lord for such a delightful addition to the special place in my heart. You want to see a picture of my granddaughter? *(Shows picture—exits.)*

Football Player *(carrying football):* I guess I represent all the people who love football and basketball and soccer and all the other sports. We have so much fun. Any spectators who get caught up in the excitement, are thrilled with watching and cheering us on. I thank God for a strong, healthy body and alert mind that helps me be a good football player. *(Exits.)*

Announcer: I can relate to many of these people. We have just heard them voice thanksgiving to a loving God who is bringing blessings to many people in many ways.

God is eternal, and I am thankful that His compassion is never removed from my life. I could hardly survive without His wonderful love and patient guidance every day of my life.

I am reminded of Scripture which is recorded in the Psalms. "Praise ye the Lord. Praise God in his sanctuary: praise him in the firmament of his power. Praise him for his mighty acts: praise him according to his excellent greatness . . . Let every thing that hath breath praise the Lord. Praise ye the Lord"

"For the Lord is good; his mercy is everlasting; and his truth endureth to all generations. . . . Enter into his gates with thanksgiving, and into his courts with praise: be thankful unto him, and bless his name."

"Sing unto the Lord with thanksgiving; sing praise . . . unto our God."

"Let the words of my mouth, and the meditation of my heart, be acceptable in thy sight, O Lord, my strength, and my redeemer." Amen.

Please stand and sing the Doxology with me. After which we will have a closing prayer.

Scripture used as follows: Psalm 150:1, 2, 6; Psalm 100:5, 4; Psalm 147:7; Psalm 19:14